COLLINS GEM
CATS
a mine of information

COLL
AST

COLLINS GEM
HORSES
& PONIES
a mine of information

COLLINS GEM
INSECTS
a mine of information

COLLINS GEM
KINGS &
QUEENS
a mine of information

COLLINS GEM
MUSHROOMS
& TOADSTOOLS
a mine of information

COLLINS GEM
SNAKES
a mine of information

COLLINS GEM
SPIDERS
a mine of information

COLLINS GEM
STRESS
Survival Guide
a mine of information

COLLINS GEM
TAROT
a mine of information

COLLINS GEM
WINE
Guide
a mine of information

COLLINS GEM
WORLD
atlas
a mine of information

COLLINS GEM
YOGA
a mine of information

COLLINS GEM
ZODIAC
Types
a mine of information

HarperCollins Publishers
PO Box, Glasgow G4 0NB

First published 1999

Reprint 10 9 8 7 6 5 4 3 2 1 0

© The Foundry Creative Media Co. Ltd, 1999 (text)

ISBN 0 00 472310-4

All pictures courtesy of Topham except: Popperfoto: pp. 47(t),
70(b), 74(t), 83(b), 85(t), 88(t), 92(r), 110(b), 133(t), 178(t);
Pictorial Press Ltd: pp. 37(b), 54(b), 56(t), 118(t), 154(r); Allsport:
pp. 112(l); Mary Evans: pp. 42(t), 108(b); Christies: pp. 12(b);
Foundry Arts: pp. 22(b), 32(b), 43(b), 44(t), 58(l), 61(b), 66(t),
141(t), 115(t), 144(b), 169(t), 171(t), 175(b), 181(b), 186(b);
Image Select: pp. 29, 82(t); London Features: pp. 39(t), 104(t),
184(t); London Transport Museum: pp. 81(t)

Created and produced by Flame Tree Publishing, part of
The Foundry Creative Media Co. Ltd
Crabtree Hall, Crabtree Lane, Fulham, London SW6 6TY

With special thanks to Josephine Cutts, Claire Dashwood,
Helen Johnson, Dave Jones and Helen Tovey

Printed in Italy by Amadeus S.p.A.

COLLINS GEM

1960s

**Nigel Gross Graeme Kay
Damian Wild Sue Wood**

HarperCollins*Publishers*

Contents

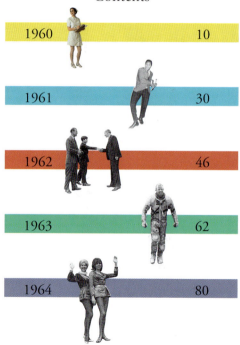

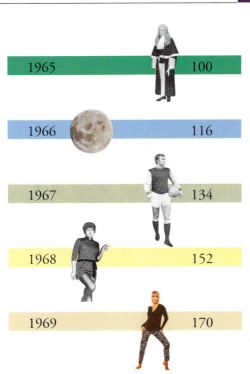

1965   100

1966   116

1967   134

1968   152

1969   170

How To Use This Book

This book covers a wide spectrum of the events that helped to define the 1960s: events of world prominence – the first hip replacement, the Vietnam War, Neil Armstrong's Moon walk – alongside those of a less portentous nature – the birth of BBC 2, the advent of topless dresses, the first fibre-tip pen. Sports, fashion, popular culture, science, fine art, the environment, literature, world news, cinema, theatre and music are all included.

1960s is divided in two ways: the contents page lists the page number at which each year of the decade begins, and every year is divided into individual months. Some months are contained on one page and some cover two pages. People, events and inventions feature within each month, providing a comprehensive look at the true spirit of the age. Every month also features a variety of entry length: some are simply a few words, some encompass several lines. In order to preserve the balance of *Zeitgeist*, every theme is afforded prominence in rotation throughout the book; as a result, not every major entry refers necessarily to an event of international significance, instead it may refer to an important fashion trend, an exciting sporting moment or the death of a leading artist. Each month also includes boxed features, which contain events that happened in the year – but not necessarily the month – in which they feature.

A comprehensive index at the end of the book assists readers who wish to look up specific entries or subjects, but who are unsure of the month or year in which they occurred.

May 1964

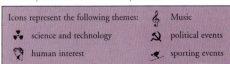

A The page number appears in a colour-coded box that indicates which year you are looking at.

B Each month is indicated at the head of the appropriate page. Some months appear on one page, some over two depending on the number of relevant entries.

C The date of the event appears at the start of the entry. Entries with no date, but which are known to have happened in the specified month, appear at the top of the list.

D Entries differ in length from a few words to several lines.

E Every page is illustrated with topical photographs or drawings.

F Tint boxes indicate events that happened in the year, but not necessarily the month, in which they feature.

Icons represent the following themes:

♪ Music

☢ science and technology

☭ political events

👩 human interest

⛷ sporting events

Introduction

The 1960s saw an incredible number of exciting new inventions, an explosion of youth freedom and culture and the culmination of the Space Race; it also saw bloody winds of change sweeping across South Africa, war between India and Pakistan, the Moors murders, the abolition of the death penalty in the UK and the deaths of several public figures, including Martin Luther King, Joe Orton, Sir Winston Churchill and John F. Kennedy.

It was a time of demonstrations, rallies and student sit-ins; of sporting triumphs and scientific breakthroughs; the Acid Tests, the Pill, Woodstock, free love and expensive drugs. If the 1950s saw the birth of the teenager, the 1960s took youth culture

to new extremes. The Beatles, Rolling Stones, Bob Dylan, Jimi Hendrix, Woodstock, the Isle of Wight Festival – all were major events that shaped their own time and, such was their influence, still do so today.

As well as the upside, the 1960s also had its downsides: such as the murderous cult of the 'Manson Family' or the many horrors experienced during the Vietnam War. Overall, it was a tumultuous decade in which both the highs and lows were monumental. This is reflected in the art and literature of the time: from the Beatles' *Sergeant Pepper's Lonely Hearts Club Band* to Benjamin Britten's *War Requiem*; from *Psycho* to *Dr No*; and from *The Grapes of Wrath* to *Private Eye*. It was a decade of discovery and disaster, of euphoria and adversity. Most important it was the decade about which everyone continues to reminisce – even those who weren't yet born.

1960

January 1960

The first effective measles vaccine is introduced in the UK, with the aim of eradicating the disease. ☢♥

A doctor demonstrates an artificial hip joint

The first hip-replacement operation has been carried out by Dr John Charnley, a surgeon with a keen interest in engineering. He fitted the device, made of plastic and stainless steel, to an arthritic patient at Wigan General Hospital. ☢

1st Cameroon gains independence from France. ☭

4th French writer **Albert Camus dies** in a car crash; he was 46. His books include *The Plague* and *The Outsider*.

All that remains of Albert Camus' car

10th Construction of the Aswan High Dam begins; Egyptian leader Colonel Nasser lays the first stone.

23rd A new depth record is set in the Marianas Trench – of 10.84 km (6.78 miles). The record was set by Jacques Piccard (France) and Donald Walsh (US) in the bathyscaphe *Trieste*.

27th The British Broadcasting Company (BBC) is to present plans for a second television channel.

BBC Television Centre

February 1960

3rd British Prime Minister Harold Macmillan angers white politicians when he tells the South African parliament of the growing 'strength of this African national consciousness'. He urges the country to move towards racial equality, saying, 'The wind of change is blowing through this continent'.

Macmillan addressing South Africa

6th Bunuel's film *Republic of Sin* premieres in Paris. It stars Gerard Philipe who tragically died from cancer in January.

14th 'Teen Angel' by Mark Denning reaches number 1 in the US.

Jean Cocteau (standing) with Pablo Picasso (far right)

18th Jean Cocteau's *Testament d' Orphee*, in which the poet plays himself, is critically slated in France.

19th Prince Andrew, the second son of the Queen and Prince Philip, is born.

27th Newsagents in Connecticut will no longer sell *Playboy*. The magazine, which is considered too pornographic, was started by millionaire Hugh Heffner. It first went on sale in 1953.

Queen Elizabeth with one-month-old Prince Andrew

1960 sees the first performance of a little-known English group called the Beatles, they play in Hamburg.

March 1960

1st British tourists are among over 12,000 people killed after an earthquake and tidal wave destroy the Moroccan resort of Agadir.

20th Lonnie Donegan's 'My Old Man's a Dustman' hits UK number 1.

21st In South Africa, the Sharpeville Massacre leaves 56 dead. A crowd of 15,000 protesters, demonstrating against new laws that require all Africans to carry ID cards, converges on a police station in the Transvaal township. Bodies scatter the ground minutes after armed police open fire.

Bodies of South Africans killed by police gunfire

April 1960

1st The US launches its first meteorological satellite: the Television and Infra Red Observation Satellite (Tiros).

9th South African Prime Minister, Hendrik Verwoerd, is shot and wounded by a white farmer.

13th Racing driver Stirling Moss is banned for a year – after being convicted for dangerous driving.

One year on: Stirling Moss regains his licence

17th Eddie Cochran dies in a car crash. After performing in Bristol, he was rushing to London for a flight to America. Gene Vincent, also in the car, was unharmed.

Satellite view of Africa, Asia and Europe

Eddie Cochran appeared in a handful of films but is best remembered for hit singles like 'Summertime Blues' and 'C'Mon Everybody'.

May 1960

A new design of 'lap and shoulder' seat belts are introduced to UK cars.

5th **The USSR** claims that the US U-2 aircraft shot down over Soviet territory was on a spying mission.

6th **Princess Margaret weds** photographer and commoner Anthony Armstrong-Jones at Westminster Abbey.

16th **British MPs support a bill** to curb the increasingly violent behaviour of Teddy boys.

Teddy boys queue for styling, shampoo and wave set

18th Real Madrid beat Eintracht Frankfurt 7–3; it is their fifth consecutive European Cup championship.

Real Madrid win again

23rd Nazi and death-camp originator Adolf Eichmann is seized in Argentina by top Israeli intelligence agents. His capture comes after a 15-year hunt. Two years later he goes on trial in Israel, where he is found guilty of being the brains behind Hitler's gas chambers, in which millions of Jews were murdered. He is sentenced to death.

31st Russian poet and author Boris Pasternak (author of *Dr Zhivago*) dies at his home in Predelkino, aged 70.

Adolf Eichmann hearing the news of his death sentence

June 1960

The first modern language laboratory opens. It will help executives working for Shell Petroleum to learn Indonesian. The lab will allow the teacher to listen in to each student's speech and offer one-to-one advice via a two-way headset.

11th **Ingrid Bergman's marriage** to Roberto Rossellini is annulled.

15th *The Apartment*, Billy Wilder's satirical take on contemporary New York life, is released in the US. The film stars Shirley MacLaine and Jack Lemmon.

15th The scars of the Hiroshima and Nagasaki bombs remain unhealed as students in Japan riot over a proposed treaty with the US.

19th The Jaguar car company merges with Daimler for a price believed to be around £3.5 million.

The classic Jaguar saloon shape.

20th US heavyweight boxer Floyd Patterson regains the world title in a rematch with Swede Ingemar Johansson.

Ingemar Johansson receives the final blow

30th After 80 years of Belgian rule, Congo finally gains independence.

Europeans flee Leopoldville for the relative safety of Brazzaville

July 1960

The English-built Electric Lightning becomes the RAF's first operational supersonic fighter.

Australian cartoonist Rolf Harris hits the UK charts with 'Tie Me Kangaroo Down Sport' and launches the wobble-board.

3rd Australian motor ace Jack **Brabham**, driving a Cooper-Climax, wins the French Grand Prix.

6th The father of the **National Health Service**, Labour MP Aneurin Bevan, dies of cancer aged 62.

7th The Hughes Corporation introduces the Light Amplification by Stimulated Emission of Radiation device. It concentrates beams of light to such an extent that holes can be drilled, even in metal – the LASER is born.

A ruby laser in use

12th Cuba wins Soviet leader Khrushchev's promise of support to expel US troops from their naval base, at Guantanamo Bay in Cuba.

21st Francis Chichester wins the first single-handed transatlantic yacht race in *Gypsy Moth III.*

21st In Ceylon (now Sri Lanka), Sirimaro Bandaranaike becomes the world's first female Prime Minister.

August 1960

The Pentel Corporation demonstrates a new type of writing implement: the fibre-tip pen.

The Edinburgh Festival witnesses the first performance of *Beyond the Fringe*.

8th **The UN orders Belgian troops** to leave Congo. They returned during riots in July – one month after Congo became independent.

10th **Alfred Hitchcock**'s chilling film, *Psycho*, starring Anthony Perkins and Janet Leigh, opens in Los Angeles.

19th **Gary Powers**, the US 'spy' pilot shot down in May, is jailed for 10 years by a Soviet court.

Anthony Perkins, in *Psycho*

Revolutionary stationery: the fibre-tip pen

Permanent Marker

25th Mao Tse-
Tung's Communist
principles are
condemned by USSR
Communists, who
cease to aid China.

**29th Prime Minister
of Jordan**, Hazza el-
Majali, is assassinated
by a bomb.

Chinese leader, Mao Tse-Tung

East-West German border blockades

**31st East Germans are
denied free travel** to the
West when the border
with West Berlin is
closed by the creation of
a partial blockade – just
one year after East
Germany applied to 60
countries for official
recognition.

The 1960 Summer Olympics are
held in Rome. 54 records are broken.

September 1960

Chubbie Checker's 'The Twist' hits US number 1.

Archaeologists replace Stonehenge's stones in their original positions

6th Archaeologists discover 10 skeletons close to Stonehenge. Initial studies point to the skeletons being around 3,800 years old, therefore dating from the Stone Age. However, the discovery still fails to shed any light on the purpose of Stonehenge.

19th Parking tickets are introduced, along with traffic wardens. In 24 hours, 344 tickets are issued.

24th The *USS Enterprise*, the world's first nuclear-powered aircraft carrier, is launched.

26th John F. Kennedy and Richard Nixon appear in the first televised debate between the US Presidential candidates.

27th A 'travelator' opens at London's Bank tube station. It is Europe's first moving pavement.

27th Estelle Sylvia Pankhurst dies. She was the daughter, and fellow campaigner, of the British suffragette leader, Emmeline Pankhurst.

Suffragette Estelle Sylvia Pankhurst

1990s traffic warden technology

29th In a display of anti-West irritation, Nikita Khrushchev interrupts Harold Macmillan's speech by banging the table – with his shoe!

October 1960

1st Nigeria becomes independent.

3rd **Brigitte Bardot** leaves hospital after recovering from a suicide attempt.

8th **Underdogs England** beat the Australians 10–3 in the Rugby League World Cup final.

9th Heavy rains cause the **worst flooding** for seven years in southern England, resulting in widespread damage.

English winger Billy Boston charges through his opponents

Soldiers help stranded motorists in Kent

11th **Freak weather claims thousands of lives** in Asia. More than 3,000 are feared dead after a 112-km/h (70-mph) cyclone hit the Ganges Delta area followed by the worst tidal wave in living memory.

20th **In a case brought by the UK government** under the Obscene Publications Act, Penguin Books Ltd goes on trial at the Old Bailey. The furore is over their intention to publish an unexpurgated, and allegedly obscene, paperback version of D. H. Lawrence's novel *Lady Chatterley's Lover*. On 2 November, the court rules that the book is not obscene.

21st **The UK's first nuclear-powered submarine**, HMS *Dreadnought*, enters service.

London's Old Bailey

November 1960

1st Plastic dustbin bags, developed by ICI, are first used by Hitchen Borough Council in Hertfordshire.

9th John F. Kennedy is elected US President, defeating Republican contender Richard Nixon.

12th The Kestrel, forerunner of the Harrier Jump Jet, makes its maiden flight.

16th US actor Clark Gable dies. He won an Academy Award for *It Happened One Night* in 1934 and was voted King of Hollywood in 1937. However, Gable is best known as Rhett Butler in *Gone With the Wind*.

Kay Williams Gable carries the flag and bible from her husband's coffin

December 1960

2nd **Vivien Leigh** ends her 21-year marriage to fellow actor Laurence Olivier.

9th **Gritty northern soap opera** *Coronation Street* appears for the first time on ITV.

20th **Richard Baer, the last commandant** of Auschwitz concentration camp, is arrested in West Germany.

Locked gates at Auschwitz

31st **The last conscripts** for the UK's National Service go on parade. Since the scheme began at the outbreak of the Second World War, a total of

5,300,000 men from all walks of life have received call-up cards. The final 2,049 recruits will be shared between the army and airforce.

1961

January 1961

3rd The US and Cuba sever all diplomatic relations.

6th Dag Hammarskjöld, the UN Secretary-General, goes to South Africa to discuss their policy of Apartheid.

6th A two-day referendum starts in France. It was proposed by Charles de Gaulle, so that Algerians can vote whether they should gain independence. This comes after six years of rebellion in Algeria.

The 100th Archbishop of Canterbury

9th The 100th Archbishop of Canterbury is appointed, Dr Michael Ramsey. He takes over from Archbishop Fisher.

10th Samuel Dashiell Hammett, whose books included the classic *The Maltese Falcon*, dies aged 64.

17th Ex-Prime Minister of Congo, Patrice Lumumba, is assassinated.

Patrice Lumumba, while he was still Prime Minister

Crowds watch the President being sworn in

20th John F. Kennedy is sworn in as the US's youngest President. He is 43 years old.

30th Conovid, the first oral female contraceptive goes on sale in the UK after exhaustive trials; so far it has close to 100% effectiveness. It is not yet available through the National Health Service.

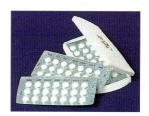

1961 sees the publication of *Catch 22* by Joseph Heller.

February 1961

The US skating team boarding their ill-fated Boeing 707

The entire US ice-skating team is killed in an aircrash in Belgium.

The first plans are announced for the 156-m (507-ft) tall GPO tower in London.

1st The first intercontinental Minuteman missile, capable of carrying nuclear warheads, is test fired by the US.

3rd Bob Dylan makes his first recordings, at a friend's house on their home equipment.

5th The UK's first automatic railway level crossing is installed near Uttoxeter.

8th After nearly 40 **years** as a radio favourite, *Children's Hour* is dropped by the BBC.

15th Soul singer **Jackie Wilson** is shot and seriously wounded by Juanita Jones, a female fan.

Teenagers rehearse for their debuts on *Children's Hour*

16th Poet and **author**, Robert Graves, whose works include *I Claudius* and *Goodbye To All That*, is appointed the new Professor of Poetry at Oxford University.

25th Elvis makes his first public stage appearance in four years, playing two shows in Memphis.

Robert Graves at a literary luncheon in London

The £20 maximum wage for English league footballers is abolished.

March 1961

6th British comedian, singer and actor George Formby dies.

8th Sir Thomas Beecham, doyen of British music, dies.

15th South Africa will leave the Commonwealth in May.

George Formby's stage personality shows even in hospital

17th Laurence Olivier marries English classical actress Joan Plowright.

21st The Beatles make their first appearance at Liverpool's Cavern Club.

20th The Royal Shakespeare Company is founded in Stratford-upon-Avon by Peter Hall and Fordham Flowers, a descendant of Charles Flowers who launched the Shakespeare Memorial Theatre in 1879.

The Royal Shakespeare Theatre and the River Avon

April 1961

The £2,196 model of Jaguar's magnificent 'E' type, rolls off the production lines. The car evolved from racing cars first produced in the early 1950s and has since been acclaimed as a style icon.

8th The Soviets continue to lead the Space Race: they have sent the first human into space. Major Yuri Gagarin reached a height of 304 km (190 miles) on his journey. The flight was a short one, lasting just 108 minutes, but was nevertheless a momentous achievement.

10th Gary Player becomes the first non-American winner of the American Masters golf tournament.

May 1961

5th **The US put their first man into space** – Alan Shepard makes a 15-minute flight.

6th **Tottenham Hotspur win** the League and FA Cup Double.

8th **Self-confessed spy George Blake** receives a record 42-year jail sentence after working as a Soviet agent.

The funeral of Gary Cooper

13th **US actor Gary Cooper dies.** His films include the Oscar winning *High Noon.*

31st **South Africa is declared a republic.** C. R. Swart is the President and the currency is the Rand. The country becomes independent of the Commonwealth after 52 per cent of the white population backed the move.

The new South African flag is hoisted

June 1961

An electric toothbrush is marketed by the Squibb Co. of New York.

6th Swiss psychoanalyst **Carl Jung** dies, aged 85. Amongst the ideas he introduced were the concepts of the extrovert and introvert.

Patsy Cline

14th Country singer Patsy Cline sustains a fractured hip and near-fatal head injuries in a car crash.

16th In a dramatic scene at Le Bourget airport, Russian dancer Rudolph Nureyev defects to the West.

July 1961

1,000 British school children are to be taught to read using an experimental 43-sound phonetic alphabet. The scheme is to happen only in selected schools to determine whether it should be adopted nationally.

2nd Ernest Hemingway dies from shotgun wounds at his Idaho home. Foul play is not suspected.

16th A train crashes near Blackpool killing six holidaymakers and injuring 116.

19th In-flight movies are introduced as a regular feature on some airlines.

August 1961

Ray Charles releases a new single, 'Hit the Road Jack'.

10th **The UK,** currently a member of the seven-nation EFTA trade alliance, applies to join the rival Common Market, also known as the European Economic Community (EEC).

30th **In France**, 63 stranded tourists are rescued after a jet plane cuts through a cable-car support. Six people die.

31st **East Germans make a last dash** for freedom as the Communist-built Berlin Wall continues to rise.

West Berliners at the Brandenburg Gate

September 1961

10th **Tragedy strikes at La Monza** as 13 spectators die when two cars leave the track.

14th **The baby-to-toddlerwear** chain, Mothercare, opens its first shop in Kingston, Surrey.

Anti-nuclear protesters are carried from Trafalgar Square

17th **London's biggest anti-nuclear protest** ends with 850 arrests, as violence erupts among the 15,000-strong crowd.

18th **The UN Secretary-General**, Dag Hammarskjöld, aged 56, is killed in an air crash. His DC6 mysteriously explodes as it is about to land at Ndola, Northern Rhodesia (now Zambia). The cause of the crash is unknown but there is speculation that sabotage was involved.

Rhodesian Police carry Dag Hammarskjöld's coffin

21st In Paris, Yves St Laurent announces plans to open his own fashion house.

25th Paul Newman makes a big cinematic impression as a mixed-up pool player in *The Hustler*.

29th A coup in Syria leads to the country breaking away from the United Arab Republic.

Screen heart throb, Paul Newman

Giant pandas are protected by the WWF

The World Wildlife Fund is established; its aims are to protect the world's endangered species and their habitats.

October 1961

The experimental US aircraft X15 breaks the 6,000-km/h (3,750-mph) barrier.

1st **Steam trains** run for the last time on the London Underground.

19th **The Art of Assemblage exhibition**, including works by Christo and Tinguely, opens in New York.

31st **The Welsh-born artist** **Augustus John dies** at the age of 83 at his home in Fordingbridge, Hampshire. John studied at the Slade School of Art and his sitters included famous literary figures such as Lady Ottoline Morrell, Thomas Hardy and Dylan Thomas.

November 1961

1st Under new legislation, immigrants will only be allowed into the UK if they can support themselves without a job; if they can prove that they have a job waiting for them; or if they have a skill that is required in the labour force.

16th The bodies of 13 Italian soldiers in the UN force are put up for sale in a Congo market.

20th *A Soldier's Prayer,* the conclusion of Kobayashi's *The Human Condition* film trilogy, opens in Tokyo.

25th The Everly Brothers enlist in the US marine corps, initially for six months' active service.

Supporters waiting to welcome immigrants to the UK

December 1961

8th **The Beach Boys** release their first record, 'Surfin', on Candix records. The American band had been known as The Pendletones until a promotion man in the record company changed their name. The first the band members knew about it was when they saw the pressed records.

9th **Tanganyika** gains independence from the UK. In 1964, with Zanzibar, it became ~~Zanzibar~~.
Tanzania

15th **Anthony Mann**'s film, *El Cid*, opens in New York.

15th **The People's Republic of China** is refused admittance to the United Nations.

Charlton Heston in the title role of *El Cid*

19th Portugal is forced to surrender Goa after Indian troops forcibly reclaim it after 400 years.

19th A hijacked US aeroplane is forced to land in Cuba. It is the first time a hijack has been carried through to completion.

Captured Portuguese soldier watched by Sikh guard

22nd A US soldier dies in South Vietnam – the first US casualty of the conflict. The US joined the war after signing a treaty with South Vietnam in July.

Active service in Vietnam

The British-made Atlas computer, the world's largest computer, is installed at Harwell atomic-research laboratory.

1962

January 1962

 Ken Kesey's *One Flew Over The Cuckoo's Nest* is published in the US.

Jack Nicholson in the film of Kesey's book

The first Rubella (German Measles) vaccine is undergoing trials in the UK.

Thalidomide, a sedative for pregnant women, is established as a cause of major malformations in babies: it is banned in many countries.

The Dow Corning Corporation of Michigan, US, announces a new development in cosmetic surgery. They have developed a plastic bag containing silicone that can be surgically implanted into a woman's breast. Once inserted, it is claimed it will be totally safe, and all but undetectable.

A smallpox vaccination clinic

14th Six people die and others become ill as smallpox breaks out in the UK.

15th UK weather reports give the temperature in both Centigrade and Fahrenheit for the first time.

15th Yves St Laurent, who started out working under Christian Dior, opens his own couture house in Paris.

Yves St Laurent surrounded by his models

February 1962

4th *The Sunday Times* releases the first issue of its colour supplement.

9th **Two people successfully climb** the Matterhorn's North Face in winter.

10th Jailed American U-2 pilot Gary Powers is freed by the Soviets in a spy swap.

The Matterhorn's imposing facade

20th John Glenn has become the first American to orbit Earth. The flight, which lasted some five hours, comes over ten months after the Soviet cosmonaut, Yuri Gagarin's, flight and well illustrates the efforts the US are making to catch up in the Space Race.

Gary Powers following his release

March 1962

The Twist Craze sweeps the US with four Twist singles in the US Top 40, including Chubby Checker's 'The Twist'. In the UK last month, an Essex schoolboy claimed a world record by dancing the Twist for 33 hours non-stop.

2nd The Congress Party, led by India's President Nehru, wins a landslide victory in the national elections.

President Nehru addresses the Congress Party

The Maltese flag

4th The British colony of Malta wins full independence, one year after the Colonial Secretary Iain Macleod announced the decision to give the Mediterranean island self-government

April 1962

2nd **After a year of waiting**, the first panda crossings open in London. These incorporate traffic lights at crossings; pedestrians can press a button to indicate that the lights should change, thus stopping the traffic and allowing them to cross.

Children investigate the new panda crossings

4th **The A6 murderer**, James Hanratty, hangs for killing a man in a lay-by at Deadman Hill, near Bedford.

12th J. **Lee Thompson**'s chilling film *Cape Fear*, starring Robert Mitchum as the villain, opens in Florida.

18th **The UK dissolves** the West Indies Federation by passing an Act of Parliament: the West Indies Act. This follows Jamaica's 1961 vote to leave the Federation.

One of Jamaica's many beaches

23rd **The UK's biggest-ever** public demonstration, organised by several groups including CND, takes place. 150,000 people, protesting against the proliferation of nuclear weapons, gather at London's Hyde Park, at the end of the annual march from Aldermaston Atomic Weapons Research Establishment.

26th **The Anglo-American satellite** *Ariel 1* is launched successfully from Cape Canaveral.

30th **Anti-establishment comedian** Peter Cook saves the satirical magazine *Private Eye*, which started in February, from folding.

Peter Cook (centre), the saviour of *Private Eye*

May 1962

Blues legend John Lee Hooker hits the UK charts for the first time with 'Boom Boom'.

9th **The Beatles sign a recording contract** with EMI's Parlophone label. Despite the band's popularity on Merseyside, the Beatles were rejected by recording label Decca earlier this year. Of the 15 songs they used at the Decca audition only three were Lennon and McCartney compositions.

11th Prince Charles starts at Gordonstoun School in Scotland.

Prince Charles meets headmaster Robert Chew

Alexander Solzhenitsyn's *One Day in the Life of Ivan Denisovich* is published in the UK.

21st John Schlesinger's film of Stan Barstow's gritty drama, *A Kind Of Loving*, opens in London.

24th The US's second astronaut, Scott Carpenter, is left for three hours floating in a raft after splashdown, having been 'lost' by mission control.

25th Benjamin Britten's latest opus, *War Requiem,* is premiered at the newly consecrated Coventry Cathedral.

31st Nazi war criminal Adolf Eichmann, designer of the Holocaust gas chambers, is executed, by hanging, in Israel.

Benjamin Britten keeping warm during rehearsals

June 1962

In the football World Cup Final, Brazil beat
Czechoslovakia 3–1.

The US's famous 12-acre penitentiary, Alcatraz

Three prisoners become the only escapees from the
notorious Californian prison of Alcatraz when they dig a
tunnel, using nail-clippers and dessert spoons, and swim
to freedom.

Author and renowned gardener, Vita Sackville-West,
dies at Sissinghurst Castle, in Kent,
aged 70.

14th Six Algerian terrorists, on a
mission to assassinate President de
Gaulle, are arrested by French police.

25th Sophia Loren's husband,
producer Carlo Ponti, may face bigamy
charges, Rome magistrates say.

Italian actress, Sophia Loren

July 1962

3rd The Algerian flag flies free in North Africa after France ends its 132-year rule.

Telstar's terrestrial reception/transmission antenna

10th *Telstar* is in orbit – the first satellite able to transmit television signals.

11th US scuba-diver Fred Baldasare becomes the first person to swim the English Channel underwater, from Cap Griz Nez in France to Sandwich in Kent.

13th UK Prime Minister **Macmillan** fires seven members of his Cabinet after a humiliating by-election defeat for the Tories.

18–20th The last Gentleman v. Players match as the MCC abolishes the distinction between amateurs and professionals.

Algerians march in celebration of their independence Day

August 1962

5th Marilyn Monroe is found dead in bed after overdosing on sleeping pills. Three-times married, former model Monroe started her career as the archetypal dumb blonde in films like *Gentlemen Prefer Blondes* and *The Seven Year Itch*. She went on to more serious roles in films like *The Misfits*.

20th West Germans stage mass protests at the Berlin Wall after a fleeing teenager is gunned down by guards.

23rd John Lennon marries Cynthia Powell in Liverpool. Paul McCartney is best man.

31st Two UK climbers, Chris Bonnington and Ian Clough, climb the Eiger's daunting north face.

Crowd and police clashes at the German border

September 1962

3rd **US novelist and poet**, e. e. cummings, dies.

8th **Venice Film Festival**'s Golden Lion is shared between Tarkovsky's *Ivan's Childhood* and Zurlini's *Family Diary*.

25th **Sonny Liston** defeats Floyd Patterson in Chicago to become the new world heavyweight boxing champion.

30th **At least three die** and 50 are injured as hate-fuelled white protesters battle to stop James Meredith being the first black student to enrol at the University of Mississippi. US President Kennedy calls in Federal Marshals to shield the student as he enters the campus.

Riots leave the campus littered with burned-out cars

October 1962

1st The first of the **James Bond films**, *Dr No*, starring Sean Connery, opens in London.

5th **The Beatles** release their first single 'Love Me Do'.

Beatles' first single

Sean Connery and Ursula Andress in *Dr No*

10th **Rock-horror single** 'Monster Mash' by Bobby 'Boris' Pickett and the Crypt-Kickers reaches number 1 in the US. The BBC bans it.

10th The US space probe *Mariner 2* finds previously unrecognised solar winds.

15th The human-rights organisation Amnesty International is founded.

22nd US President Kennedy blockades Cuba when Soviet missiles are discovered there.

22nd Traitor William Vassall is jailed for 18 years for spying for the Soviets during an Admiralty posting.

28th Cuban missile crisis ends as Khrushchev decides to withdraw Soviet missiles from the island.

William Vassall returns to Wormwood Scrubs Prison

31st The New Realists exhibition including works from Claes Oldenberg, James Rosenquist, Christo, Yves Klein and Andy Warhol opens at the Sidney Janis Gallery, New York.

Communication engineers monitor the progress of *Mariner 2*

November 1962

1st The Soviets launch the first interplanetary probe towards Mars.

2nd Spy suspect Greville Wynne is seized by the KGB. The British businessman is flown to Moscow for questioning after his arrest in Budapest amid Soviet accusations of espionage. Wynne was, ostensibly, in Hungary to exhibit at a trade fair.

Greville Wynne, accused of espionage

7th Freedom fighter Nelson Mandela is sentenced to five years in prison – for inciting strikes, leaving South Africa illegally and for not carrying ID.

Nelson Mandela, sentenced to five years in prison

December 1962

4th Two divers from the UK set a new depth record for scuba-diving. Using the latest equipment to offset the effects of depth sickness, which mimics drunkenness, they manage to reach a depth of just over 300 m (1,000 ft).

10th American author John Steinbeck, whose works include *The Grapes of Wrath*, wins the Nobel Prize for Literature.

Author John Steinbeck at a press conference

16th Anglo-French talks over the UK's proposed entry

into the Common Market end in stalemate.

The modern flag of the European Union

1963

January 1963

The tape player/recorder is announced by Phillips; it will use a handy 'cassette' rather than bulky reels.

8th Moscow hosts the **premiere** of Shostakovich's opera *Katerina Izmalovia* (an updating of the play *Lady Macbeth of Mtsensk*).

11th *Summer Holiday*, Cliff Richard's fourth film, premieres in London and South Africa.

Russian composer, Dmitri Shostakovich

17th Homes **and businesses** are plunged into darkness as industrial action by UK power workers causes blackouts.

The Electricity Council meets in darkness during a power cut

The *Mannequin Pis*, Brussels

17th Students in Brussels steal the statue of the *Mannequin Pis*.

18th British Labour party leader and moderate socialist Hugh Gaitskell dies aged 56, after a short illness.

Kim Philby's deserted office desk

23rd Former British diplomat 'Kim' Philby has disappeared. The ex-MI5 officer was working in Beirut at the time of his disappearance. In 1955, Philby denied accusations that he was a Communist or that he was involved in the disappearance of spies Burgess and McLean.

Britain has its coldest January and February since 1740.

February 1963

2nd **Janis Joplin is arrested** for shoplifting in Berkeley, USA. Young folk singer Joplin recently dropped out of college and moved to San Francisco where she has been singing in local clubs.

9th **The first test flight** of Boeing's new airliner, the 727, is completed successfully.

11th US poet Sylvia Plath commits suicide.

14th **At Leeds General Infirmary**, a kidney from a dead man has successfully been transplanted into a living patient.

14th **Harold Wilson** is elected leader of the UK's Labour Party.

American singer Janis Joplin

March 1963

5th Country singer **Patsy Cline** is killed in a plane crash in Tennessee with Cowboy Copas and Hawkshaw Hawkins. Patsy was born in 1932 and began singing as a child. She made her first professional appearance in 1952. Her most famous hit is the now-classic 'Crazy'.

21st The London Underground acquires its first fully automatic trains.

27th The Beeching Report recommends closing over 2,000 British railway stations, and a quarter of all passenger railway lines.

30th The Crystals reach number 1 with the Phil Spector-produced 'He's So Fine'.

April 1963

Alfred Hitchcock's avian thriller film, *The Birds*, is playing to packed audiences throughout New York.

4th The Beatles' 'Can't Buy Me Love' knocks their 'She Loves You' off the top of the US charts – their 'I Wanna Hold Your Hand' was the previous number 1.

8th David Lean's epic film *Lawrence of Arabia* wins seven Oscars.

Peter O' Toole and Omar Sharif in *Lawrence of Arabia*

12th Black civil-rights leader Martin Luther King is arrested. Fighting erupts in Birmingham, Alabama, after King and fellow race campaigner Ralph Abernathy are seized by police during a peaceful march against segregation. Both face charges of parading without permission.

16th The Russian pianist Vladimir Ashkenazy asks for, and is granted, political asylum in the UK.

The Second Vatican Council approves the use of vernacular language in Mass, rather than the traditional Latin.

Pop Artist Roy Lichtenstein exhibits *Whaam!*.

May 1963

The Organization of African Unity is founded.

Mississippi bluesman Elmore James dies aged 45. His distinctive guitar style was widely copied; Eric Clapton and George Harrison are numbered among his admirers.

7th The US has launched its second *Telstar* communications satellite on schedule.

11th Soviet traitor Penkovsky is sentenced to death and British go-between Wynne is jailed by a Moscow court.

15th Two years after they became the first English team this century to win 'the double' of FA Cup and League Championship Tottenham Hotspur, inspired by Danny Blanchflower, become the first British side to win the European Cup when they beat Atletico Madrid 5-1 in Rotterdam.

Danny Blanchflower held aloft by the Spurs' team

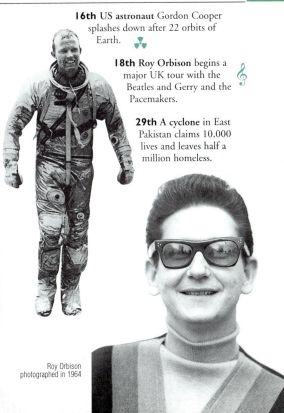

16th US astronaut Gordon Cooper splashes down after 22 orbits of Earth.

18th Roy Orbison begins a major UK tour with the Beatles and Gerry and the Pacemakers.

29th A cyclone in East Pakistan claims 10,000 lives and leaves half a million homeless.

Roy Orbison
photographed in 1964

June 1963

5th War Minister John **Profumo** resigns after admitting lying about his relationship with Christine Keeler.

16th Soviet cosmonaut Valentina Tereshkova becomes the first woman to go into space.

18th At Wembley, British boxer Henry Cooper knocks down Cassius Clay, but loses when the fight is stopped.

21st Cardinal Giovanni Battista Montini is elected Pope Paul VI following the death of the much-loved liberal Pope John XXIII from cancer. Pope Paul VI plans to continue along his predecessor's path to attain Christian unity.

July 1963

A hydrofoil of the 1970s

8th **The first hydrofoil** crossing of the English Channel occurs – the *Aquavit* travels between Ostend and London.

10th Lawrence Alloways' Six Painters and An Object exhibition, featuring works from Roy Lichtenstein, Jim Dine, Jasper Johns, Richard Rauschenberg, Jim Rosenquist and Andy Warhol, opens at the Los Angeles County Museum.

31st Osteopath Dr Stephen Ward takes a fatal overdose as a vice jury blames him for the Profumo scandal. He dies on 3 August.

31st Viscount Stansgate renounces his title to become Anthony Wedgewood Benn, in order to stand as an MP.

Stephen Ward on his way to the Old Bailey

August 1963

5th Craig Breedlove breaks the 640 km/h (400 mph) land-speed barrier – but it is not officially ratified.

Train robbery suspects escorted into court

8th A special Post Office train, carrying old bank-notes due for incineration, is hijacked at Cheddington, Buckinghamshire, by an armed, masked gang. The raiders take an estimated £2.6 million in their well-planned raid. The train's driver Jack Mills receives very severe head injuries.

8th A Nuclear-test ban treaty is signed by the US, UK and USSR. It bans tests in the atmosphere, in space and under water.

9th The first edition of television pop show *Ready Steady Go* goes out. Billy Fury is the main guest.

15th Three Bristol footballers confess to taking bribes and are banned for life by the FA.

26th The West Indies defeat England by 8 wickets to take the Test series 3–1.

28th Black civil-rights leader Luther King tells 200,000 supporters: 'I have a dream...' at the largest rally yet in Washington, DC.

30th A telephone hotline is established between the White House and the Kremlin.

Martin Luther King at the Lincoln Memorial

September 1963

4th Ronnie Biggs, one of the Great Train robbers, is arrested.

7th The Final of the first limited-over cricket contest takes place – Sussex beat Warwickshire in the Gillette Cup.

9th Scottish driver Jim Clark wins the British Grand Prix

Suspect Ronnie Biggs with police detectives

and, at 27, becomes the youngest Formula 1 World Champion.

15th Anti-black tempers flare in Birmingham, Alabama and a black church is bombed – many people are burned to death.

A triumphant Jim Clark

A £43-million missile early-warning system

17th A radar system to warn the UK of missile attack opens at Flyingdales. ☢

18th The UN imposes sanctions on South Africa – banning the export of arms and petroleum to the country – because of Apartheid.

19th The UK and France plan to build a Channel Tunnel (it does not come to fruition for over 30 years).

South Africans protest against racism

20th Professor George Green has completed the world's first blood transfusion to an unborn baby. This miracle of modern science was carried out at the National Women's Hospital, Auckland, New Zealand.

The publication of Rachel Carson's *Silent Spring* signals the beginning of environmental awareness.

October 1963

A patent has been granted to the Flymo company for a new type of lawnmower inspired by the hovercraft.

1st Dr Nnamdi Azikiwe is named first premier of a new republic of Nigeria.

Dr Azikiwe, Premier of the Nigerian Senate

1st Artist George Baselitz is accused of obscenity at an exhibition in Berlin.

7th Tony Richardson's film of Henry Fielding's *Tom Jones* starring Albert Finney opens in New York.

The screen adaptation of *Tom Jones*

12th Chanteuse Edith Piaf dies. Moving from the streets to cabaret halls, Piaf was famous for her sad, nostalgic songs about life on the streets. She suffered a severe illness two years ago and despite a return to the stage it proved to be short-lived.

14th The US airlines Pan-Am and TWA place orders for 21 supersonic jet airliners.

18th Lord Home is the new British Prime Minister after Harold Macmillan resigns from his hospital bed. On 23 October, Lord Home renounces his title to become Sir Alec Douglas Home.

William Hartnell: the first Dr Who

Dr Who appears on British television screens for the first time.

November 1963

4th The Beatles appear on Royal Variety show. John Lennon says: 'Those of you in the cheaper seats clap, the rest of you rattle your jewellery'.

22nd Lone gunman assassinates John F. Kennedy, the US's 35th President. JFK, 46, is shot in the head as he and his wife Jackie are driven through Dallas, Texas, in an open-top car. After surgeons lose their fight to

save Kennedy's life, Lyndon Johnson is hastily sworn in as President. Police arrest suspect Lee Harvey Oswald. On 24 November, Oswald is shot by Jack Ruby while under police escort.

22nd Author Aldous Huxley, whose works include *Brave New World* and *Island*, dies aged 69.

Huxley at the International Congress of Psychology

December 1963

Singer and actor Frank Sinatra is kidnapped at gunpoint, but is released after 36 hours.

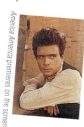

America America premieres on the screen

Film premieres: Stanley Donen's *Charade* (5th), Elia Kazan's *America America* (16th) and Jean-Luc Godard's *Contempt (le Mepris)* (20th).

12th **Kenya gains independence** as the Duke of Edinburgh hands over the control to former Mau Mau leader Jomo Kenyatta.

21st **An under-pitch heating system** is installed at the Leeds Rugby League ground to allow (nearly) all-weather play.

23rd **A blaze on the Atlantic cruise ship**, *Lakonia*, kills 117; a further 919 passengers are plucked to safety.

The Union Jack is lowered for the last time in Kenya

1964

January 1964

The Sharp Company of Japan reveals its new desk-top electronic calculator.

Anti-American feeling causes riots in Panama – diplomatic relations are severed.

Barbara Hulanicki's Biba boutique in Kensington starts attracting visitors from around the world looking for innovative fashions, especially skin-tight clothes and muted colours exploiting Hollywood glamour and Art Deco pastiche. The label started out as a mail-order business before its move to London.

The Biba make-up look

4th Pope Paul VI visits the Holy Land on a pilgrimage.

High security surrounds the Pope's visit

London Underground now has fully automatic ticket barriers

5th The **London Underground** now has automatic ticket barriers as well as trains.

20th British forces put down uprisings in East Africa: Tanganyika (now Tanzania), Kenya and Uganda.

22nd Northern Rhodesia sees Kenneth Kaunda sworn in as the nation's first Prime Minister. The country is renamed Zambia in August.

The swearing-in of Kenneth Kaunda

February 1964

1st **Governor of Indiana** declares the Kingsmen's 'Louie Louie' pornographic, though the lyrics are barely distinguishable.

Earth-rise, seen from the Moon

3rd The US rocket *Ranger 3* crashes into the Moon – as intended – but fails to send back the hoped-for pictures.

10th In the UK, all copies of the novel *Fanny Hill* are to be seized after being declared obscene.

19th British comedian Peter Sellers marries actress Brit Ekland.

Soldiers destroy Turkish Cypriot barricades

19th Cypriot crisis over warring Turks and Greeks. As fighting on the island grows more fierce with casualties reported on both sides, the UK sends in 1,500 reinforcements for British troops already trying to negotiate a cease-fire.

25th In Florida underdog Cassius Clay beats Sonny Liston to take the world heavyweight boxing title.

26th Five Polaris nuclear-missile submarines are to provide the bulk of the UK's future nuclear deterrent.

The 18th Summer Olympics are held in Tokyo. Japan win 16 gold medals, beaten only by the US and USSR.

March 1964

John Lennon publishes *In His Own Write* and is immediately compared to James Joyce.

20th Irish playwright and rabble-rouser Brendan Behan dies from alcohol poisoning at the age of 41.

28th The pirate station **Radio Caroline** begins broadcasting from a ship in the North Sea.

John Lennon

30th Mods and Rockers clash on Clacton beach. Police fear the clash will herald a summer of violence. Local hoteliers call for an inquiry into the hooliganism after 100 youths, most of whom have travelled up from London for the Bank Holiday weekend, are arrested.

April 1964

The UK's first regular passenger-carrying hydrofoil service opens between the Channel Islands and France.

16th Great Train Robbery jury convicts Biggs. Twelve members of the gang, including Ronnie Biggs, are found guilty of holding up a train carrying £2.6 million in mailbags and of attacking the driver. They are sentenced to a total of 307 years in jail. Police have yet to trace 20 others still on the run.

Ronald Biggs leaving
Aylesbury police station

21st *Play School* is the first programme broadcast on the new television channel BBC 2.

May 1964

11th **The US's new 3,200-km/h** (2,000-mph) bomber, the B70 Valkyrie, makes its first flight.

The XB70, built a few months after the B70

14th **Egyptian leader Nasser** and Soviet chief Khrushchev agree to re-route the Nile to make way for the Aswan High Dam.

14th **Jacques Demy's** unusual musical *Les Parapluies de Cherbourg* wins the Grand Prix at Cannes.

Starlets pose at the Cannes Film Festival

Malta and Nyasaland (now Malawi) both gain independence from the UK.

17th **Bob Dylan plays his first major UK concert** at the Royal Festival Hall. Heavily influenced by Woody Guthrie, Dylan's folk songs like 'Blowin' in the Wind' and 'The Times They Are a Changin'' are noted for his unconventional vocal style and lyrics that tackle social and political issues.

18th **Mods and Rockers** clash again at Margate and other south-coast resorts.

24th **Rioting causes 135 deaths** during an international football game between Peru and Argentina.

28th **Nehru**, India's Prime Minister since independence in 1947, dies of a heart attack.

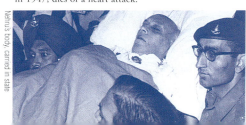

Nehru's body, carried in state

June 1964

3rd **After 12 unsuccessful attempts** the jockey Scobie Breasley, riding Santa Claus, finally wins the Derby.

4th **The UK's missile Blue Streak** has its first test firing at Woomera, Australia.

9th **Newspaper tycoon Lord Beaverbrook**, born William Maxwell Aitken, dies of cancer aged 85. The owner of the *Daily Express*, *Evening Standard* and the *Sunday Express* made his fortune as a stockbroker and later served in the governments of Lloyd George and Winston Churchill.

Lord Beaverbrook (left) in his days as a media giant

11th **Greece and Turkey** reach stalemate over Cyprus.

Nelson Mandela during his imprisonment

Top of the Pops, the show that presents the chart's hottest new entries, debuts on BBC television.

14th Nelson Mandela **is sentenced to life** and sent to Robben Island Jail, for plotting to overthrow the South African government.

Peter Sellers as Inspector Clouseau

24th *A Shot In The Dark* the sequel to *The Pink Panther* opens in New York. The first film was released in 1963 and memorably starred Peter Sellers as Inspector Clouseau; David Niven co-starred.

29th IBM **markets** the first practical word processor. Capable of making corrections, it has magnetic tape storage.

A 1970s IBM computer – a far cry from the word processor

July 1964

2nd US President **Johnson** signs a historic Civil Rights Act in his first major move to end racial discrimination.

6th The Beatles' first film, *A Hard Day's Night*, directed by Richard Lester, opens in London.

11th British rhythm-and-blues band, The Animals, hit number 1 with 'House of the Rising Sun'.

This year, for the first time, women are allowed to vote in Chile.

17th Donald Campbell, son of the late Sir Malcolm Campbell sets a new land-speed record of 644 km/h (403.10 mph).

29th The first Brook advisory clinic opens in London. The clinic will provide advice on contraception and family planning to unmarried couples with a particular emphasis on the young. Its opening is a source of some controversy.

31st The US space probe *Ranger 7* transmits the first close-up pictures of the Moon.

31st Country-music star Jim Reeves dies in an aircrash aged 40. His hits included 'He'll Have A Go'.

Jim Reeves

The Animals performing in 1965

August 1964

7th Congress gives President Johnson backing to take 'all necessary action' against North Vietnam after US bombing raids.

12th Ian Fleming, the man who created James Bond, dies of a heart attack at the age of 56.

Ian Fleming at his chambers in the Inner Temple

21st Three women are prosecuted for indecency for wearing topless dresses on Westminster Bridge. It is a fashion that is catching on in the capital this summer. The opening of the film *London in the Raw* emphasises this trend.

September 1964

4th **The Forth Road Bridge** in Scotland is officially opened. Its central span alone is over 395 m (1,300 ft) long, making it the UK's longest bridge and the sixth longest in the world. It cost just under £11 million to build.

Tabloid newspaper *The Sun* is first published.

27th **The UK fighter aircraft TSR 2** has its first flight.

The approach to the Firth of Forth bridge

27th **The Warren Commission** report on Kennedy's killing pinpoints failings by the FBI and Secret Service, but no conspiracy.

28th Harpo Marx, the silent member of the team of comic brothers, dies aged 70.

US President, John F. Kennedy

October 1964

13th The first spacecraft to carry a three-man crew returned safely to Earth today. It was launched by the USSR.

14th Martin Luther King wins the Nobel Peace Prize.

Civil Rights leader Martin Luther King

15th US composer Cole Porter, who penned stage classics like 'Begin the Beguine', dies.

15th Khrushchev loses top job while on holiday. The Soviet leader, unopposed for six years, is at his Black Sea villa when a well-organised Kremlin coup deposes him. He returns to Moscow and is sent into retirement as Leonid Brezhnev replaces him as Communist Party leader.

16th China explodes its first atomic bomb and becomes the fifth member of the 'Nuclear Club'.

Leonid Brezhnev at Palmiro Togliatti's funeral

16th Labour ends 13 years of Tory rule in the UK after scraping through to an election victory. Harold Wilson becomes Prime Minister, with a majority of four.

21st The big-screen version of *My Fair Lady*, starring Audrey Hepburn, opens in New York.

29th Dorothy Hodgkin wins the Nobel Prize for Chemistry, for her work on understanding the structure of complex molecules.

Harold Wilson

November 1964

King Saud of Saudi Arabia is deposed by his brother Faisal.

24-year-old former marine, Lee Harvey Oswald

The Warren Report in the US finds that JFK's assassin, Lee Harvey Oswald, acted alone.

1st Hostilities escalate in Vietnam. The US base of Bien Hoa in South Vietnam comes under heavy fire in a major assault by Communist Vietcong, destroying six US planes. South Vietnamese forces retaliate with US helicopter support in the biggest strike yet on the known Communist base near Saigon.

2nd The first episode of *Crossroads*, a soap opera set in a Midlands motel, is broadcast on British television.

American troops in Vietnam

3rd US President Johnson (LBJ), sworn in after Kennedy's assassination, stays in power with an election landslide.

17th The UK declares it will ban the export of arms to South Africa over the country's continued system of Apartheid.

30th Terry Downes retires after losing his world light-heavyweight boxing title in Manchester.

US President Lyndon Baines Johnson

Downes opens a betting shop after retiring

December 1964

2nd The Pope's visit to Bombay draws crowds of two million.

8th Lord Marks, of Marks and Spencer, dies. He was a pioneer of affordable, good-quality clothes.

10th The French existentialist author Jean Paul Sartre wins the Nobel Prize for Literature.

12th Soul star Sam Cooke is shot dead by a hotel manageress who claims he attacked her and tried to rape a young woman. With hits like 'Wonderful World', Cooke was probably the most successful soul singer of the last 10 years.

Author Jean Paul Sartre

21st The UK death penalty for murder ceases after British MPs vote 355 to 170 for abolition.

27th The Supremes make their first TV appearance on the *Ed Sullivan Show*.

31st Donald Campbell sets a new speed record. Again in Australia, this time it is on water and at 422.1 km/h (276.33 mph).

The Supremes: Diana Ross, Mary Wilson and Cindy Birdsong

1964 Films:

Dr Strangelove
Eight and a Half
A Fistful of Dollars
Lord of the Flies

1965

January 1965

Poet and playwright T. S. **Eliot**, whose works included *The Waste Land*, dies aged 76.

1st Stanley **Matthews** is the first footballer to receive a knighthood.

2nd Indonesia becomes the first country to leave the UN.

The Maldive Islands and the Gambia gain independence from Britain.

Adam Faith in What A Whopper

8th Singer Adam Faith cancels his South African gigs after being told he cannot perform to multi-racial audiences.

14th The two Prime Ministers of **Ireland** (North and South) meet in Ireland for the first time since the Partition.

20th Alan Freed, the DJ credited with coining the term 'Rock and Roll', dies.

30th Former British Prime Minister, Sir Winston Churchill, is buried after almost a week of national mourning. He died aged 90. Churchill was often described as 'the greatest living Englishman' as much for his powerful style of oratory as for his inspirational prime-ministerial leadership during the Second World War. He sat in the House of Commons for 60 years.

February 1965

1st P. J. Proby is banned by ABC Theatres after splitting his trousers while performing in two of their theatres.

8th UK government imposes cigarette-advertising ban on television, but lets newspaper adverts continue.

11th Beatles' drummer Ringo Starr weds Liverpool hairdresser Maureen Cox.

15th US singer Nat King Cole dies of lung cancer.

21st American black Muslim leader Malcolm X is shot dead in New York. Founder of the Organisation for Afro-American Unity after

converting to the black Muslim sect led by Elijah Muhammad, Malcolm X pressed for black separatism and advocated violence in self-defence. He was assassinated by black Muslim opponents while speaking in Harlem.

22nd The new UK strike fighter, the TSR 2, is beginning to live up to its promise and today broke the sound barrier for the first time. It managed this despite engine troubles! Everything is looking good for full production by the middle of next year.

23rd Lancashire-born Stan Laurel, the skinny half of the Laurel and Hardy comedy partnership, dies.

March 1965

Eric Clapton with the Yardbirds

Eric 'Slowhand' Clapton leaves the Yardbirds after 18 months.

9th The first effective talking computer is introduced in the New York Stock Exchange. It has a 126-word vocabulary. ☢

18th Colonel Alexei Leonev is the first man to 'walk' in space. The Colonel remained outside his *Voshkod 2* spacecraft for just under 10 minutes, during which time he even managed a somersault. Yet again the Soviets have set a new first in the Space Race.

28th The FBI, police and troops protect 25,000 black civil-rights marchers led by Martin Luther King.

April 1965

6th Twins Reggie and Ronnie Kray, leaders of a notorious gang, walk free from a London court at the end of a month-long trial. The jury found them not guilty of running a protection racket. The brothers were arrested in January 1965 on suspicion of demanding money with menaces.

6th The first commercial telecommunications satellite, the *Early Bird*, is launched from Cape Kennedy.

Early Bird, simultaneously handles up to 480 calls

27th European peace protesters take to the streets because of the US's growing involvement in the Vietnam War.

The Kray Twins with brother, Charles

May 1965

12th The Soviet unmanned spacecraft *Luna 5* fails in its mission to land on the Moon.

13th Arab states sever diplomatic links with West Germany after Bonn reveals good relations with Israel.

17th NBC has made use of the *Early Bird* satellite to transmit the first transatlantic colour TV programme. The half-hour show, *A New Look at Olde England*, was a potted history of the UK for the US viewer.

31st Jim Clark in a Lotus becomes the first foreigner to win the US Indianapolis 500.

June 1965

'Hands Free' landing made by computer

10th A BEA Trident airliner has made the world's first operational landing on auto-pilot. The airliner touched down at Heathrow airport after a flight from Paris with no assistance from the pilot. BEA has assured its pilots that the system is there to help them rather than replace them!

14th Two OBEs are returned to the Queen in protest at the award of MBEs to The Beatles.

29th US troops go on the attack for the first time in a joint operation with the South Vietnamese.

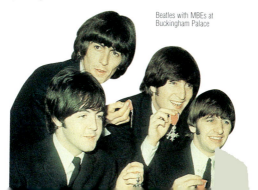

Beatles with MBEs at Buckingham Palace

July 1965

15th The US space probe *Mariner 4* has reached Mars and is transmitting back the first close-up pictures of the enigmatic red planet. Launched last November the journey has taken nearly nine months. Hopefully the pictures will solve the mystery surrounding the canals criss-crossing the planet's surface once and for all.

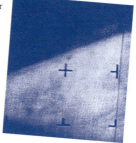

20th A Bill to end the UK's death **penalty** is given surprise support by a majority in the House of Lords.

27th Edward Heath becomes leader of the Tory Party.

30th *Coronation Street* is Britain's most popular television programme.

August 1965

10th Kim Philby, the 'third man' in the Burgess-MacLean spy ring, loses his OBE.

12th The first female High Court judge is appointed: 60-year-old Elizabeth Lane, a barrister since 1940. Lane has already been the first female county court judge, the first woman divorce commissioner and the first woman to preside over one of the Courts of the Inner London Sessions.

18th Photographer David Bailey weds French actress Catherine Deneuve. Mick Jagger is best man.

21st Charlton's Keith Peacock is the first footballer to be used under the new rules regarding substitutes.

27th Pioneering architect Le Corbusier dies.

Catherine Deneuve and David Bailey in London

September 1965

A map claimed to have been drawn by Vikings some 1,000 years ago clearly shows the eastern seaboard of the US. It has long been claimed that Viking explorers discovered America long before Columbus. However, forgery has not yet been ruled out.

1st Pakistan breaches Kashmir boundaries leading to a new phase in the India/Pakistan conflict. Kashmir was divided between India and Pakistan in 1949.

4th Albert Schweitzer dies. Dr Schweitzer, a Nobel Peace Prizewinner, devoted much of his life to the people of Africa and is buried in Lambaréné (now in Gabon).

22nd Rival claims over Kashmir threaten world peace as Pakistan and India go to war.

The Mini has become a British icon

Pakistani soldiers outside captured Indian frontier post

29th **Aston Martin** have revealed their new car, the DB 6, the follow-up to the celebrated DB5. Production of the DB5, best known as the car driven by James Bond, has now ceased.

29th The Who release 'My Generation' backed by 'Shout and Shimmy'.

30th EMI starts selling LPs, through 3,000 grocers, at 12s/6d.

British band, the Who

1965 sees the one millionth Mini drive on to the streets.

October 1965

7th Golf's biennial **Ryder Cup** tournament between the UK and the US begins at Royal Birkdale.

7th **The UK's tallest building**, the 188-m (620-ft) Post Office Tower, is opened by Prime Minister Harold Wilson.

17th Concurrent anti-Vietnam demonstrations are held in the UK and US.

19th In the US, a public hearing is held concerning the murderous racist group, the Ku-Klux-Klan.

The notorious
Moors Murderers

24th Benjamin Britten's *Voices For Today* is premiered simultaneously in Paris, New York and London.

28th Moors murderers Ian Brady, 27, and girlfriend Myra Hindley, 23, appear in a Cheshire court charged with the murder of 10-year-old Lesley Ann Downey. A police search revealed her body on Saddleworth Moor two weeks ago. The search continues for more bodies.

30th 'Friendly' fire kills 48 as US planes bomb the wrong Vietnamese village.

Vietnamese villagers flee their homes

Queen Elizabeth II unveils a three-acre memorial garden in Surrey. It is dedicated to the memory of murdered US President John F. Kennedy.

November 1965

Jean Shrimpton causes a scandal when she appears at the Melbourne Gold Cup, Australia's premier horse-racing event, with a skirt four inches above the knee.

Rhodesian Prime Minister, Ian Smith

11th Rebel Southern Rhodesia breaks from the UK. Prime Minister Ian Smith makes an expected, but illegal, unilateral declaration of independence (UDI) causing international uproar. Rhodesia, the last British colony in Africa, remains under white rule, with no say to its four million black inhabitants.

29th The National Viewers and Listeners Association is set up in the UK by moral crusader Mary Whitehouse.

Mary Whitehouse's petition against 'BBC Dirt'

December 1965

The Beatles release their new album *Rubber Soul*. The sound is more experimental than the pure pop of their previous LPs.

16th Author William Somerset Maugham dies, aged 91, at his home in Cap Ferrat, France.

22nd Broadcaster Richard Dimbleby, who covered all the major Royal events for the BBC, dies of cancer aged 52.

24th Peace reigns over war-torn Vietnam as both sides respect a Christmas truce.

Richard Dimbleby at his *Panorama* desk

1966

January 1966

Despite the fact that it is soon to become an illegal substance, the use of the hallucinogenic drug LSD continues to rise in US. Originally conceived as a treatment for the mentally ill and alcoholics, the drug's popularity with the 'hippie' generation is booming.

Paul Simon and Art Garfunkel

1st The *Sounds of Silence* LP by Simon and Garfunkel reaches number 1 in the US.

1st The **British Board** of Film Classification (BBFC) is set up in London.

Archive film stored in canisters

10th The UK has its first **push-button phones** as they go into service at the Langham exchange in London.

An early push-button telephone

19th Nehru's daughter, Mrs Indira Gandhi, promises a 'climate of peace' as the new Indian Prime Minister.

21st George Harrison marries Pattie Boyd. They met on the set of *A Hard Day's Night* in 1964.

29th The 'Breath Test' arrives for UK motorists in an important attempt to cut down on the accidents caused by drink-driving.

George Harrison is the third Beatle to marry

February 1966

Buster Keaton

1st US actor and director Buster Keaton, star of the silent screen, dies at 70.

3rd The Soviet *Luna 9* has made a soft landing on the Moon and is sending back pictures to Earth.

8th Freddie Laker establishes his own air-line promising 'cheaper and longer holidays' for his customers.

14th Russians Andrey Sinyasky and Yuri Daniel are imprisoned for smuggling their banned books to the West.

Freddie Laker standing by his new aircraft

March 1966

Five climbers have conquered the Eiger by the direct north-face route.

Beatles singer and writer, John Lennon

4th 'We are more popular than Jesus,' the Beatles' John Lennon tells the *Evening Standard.*

23rd Rome witnesses the first official meeting of the Pope and the Archbishop of Canterbury for 400 years.

27th The stolen World Cup trophy is found in South London by a mongrel dog called Pickles. The coveted Jules Rimet prize was unearthed in the garden of Pickles's owner, David Corbett. The solid gold trophy was stolen from a London exhibition on 20 March.

April 1966

1st **Harold Wilson is jubilant** after a decisive election win gives Labour a 96-seat majority.

4th The Soviet space craft *Luna 10* goes into orbit round the Moon.

5th **Shell Oil** anounces the discovery of oil off the coast near Great Yarmouth.

7th The US H-bomb that 'fell off' a B52 bomber in February is found.

Great Yarmouth Harbour

10th Novelist and biographer **Evelyn Waugh** dies at the age of 62 at his home in Somerset. The son of a publisher and literary critic, the author was a practising Catholic and his later works, including *The Loved One*, often reflected his religious beliefs.

15th *Time* magazine describes London as the 'swinging city'.

19th Australians are to **fight** alongside Americans as the first troops set off for Vietnam.

30th A regular **passenger hovercraft** service commences between Ramsgate and Calais.

Australian troops join in the Vietnam war

The first episodes of *Thunderbirds* are transmitted on ITV. The show goes on to achieve cult status.

May 1966

1st The Beatles and the Stones play the *NME* poll-winners' party at the Empire Pool, Wembley.

6th Moors Murderers Brady and Hindley are jailed for life after an all-male jury convicts them of brutal child murders.

A US soldier avoids confrontation with protesters

15th Anti-war demonstrators make a bid for peace at Washington. The White House wakes up to a mass gathering, as 8,000 protesters link hands to form a human ring around the Presidential base. Their two-hour protest is about US intervention in Vietnam.

30th Following in the tyre tracks of Jim Clark, Graham Hill wins the Indianapolis 500 race.

Graham Hill at Brands Hatch

June 1966

Bob Dylan

1st At his concert at the Royal Albert Hall, Bob Dylan horrifies fans by using an electric back-up band and is heckled.

1st **Philips Petroleum** has discovered another enormous oil field in the North Sea.

2nd **Eamon de Valera**, President of Ireland, dies.

Benjamin Britten

3rd **Benjamin Britten**'s *The Golden Vanity*, featuring the Vienna Boys' Choir receives its world premiere at Snape Maltings. The words are supplied by Colin Graham. On-stage effects include the sound of splashing water and cannon fire.

29th **Barclays Bank** launches Barclaycard, the UK's first plastic form of currency.

July 1966

7th Warsaw Pact nations offer extra manpower to strengthen North Vietnam's fighting position.

14th Brigitte Bardot weds Günther Sachs while, on the 19th, Frank Sinatra marries Mia Farrow in Las Vegas.

Brigitte Bardot and Günther Sachs in Bavaria

17th In Berkeley, California, teenager Jim Ryun sets a new world record for the mile: 3 mins, 51.3 secs.

20th Wilson grimly **announces** a six-month pay and price freeze in the UK to curb runaway inflation.

23rd US actor Montgomery Clift dies. He was the star of films like *A Place in the Sun* and *From Here to Eternity*. Clift, a homosexual, was never a comfortable film star. He delayed his move from stage to screen and later turned down many promising roles.

30th In a dramatic game that goes to extra time the host nation England defeat West Germany 4-2 to win the football World Cup at Wembley. West Ham's Geoff Hurst becomes the first man to score a hat-trick in a World Cup final.

Bobby Moore holding the World Cup

August 1966

13th **Impassioned bands** of Red Guard students spread Chairman Mao's Cultural Revolution across China.

14th **Just behind the Soviets**, the US *Orbiter 1* achieves lunar orbit.

22nd **Plans are unveiled** for a new 34-storey London skyscraper; it will be named Centre Point.

27th **The Beach Boys'** single 'God Only Knows' hits number 2 in the UK charts.

The Beach Boys on stage

More and more skyscrapers break London's skyline

September 1966

6th Architect of Apartheid, Prime Minister Dr Hendrik Verwoerd, is knifed to death in the South African House of Assembly.

South African military leaders carry Verwoerd's coffin

18th The first **experimental** use of aerofoils on a racing car takes place.

25th British circus owner Billy Smart dies.

28th Poet André Breton dies aged 70. Breton was interested in psychoanalysis and experimented with automatic writing as a means of artistic expression. The word chosen to describe this technique was *surrealisme*. In 1924 he published the First Surrealist Manifesto and an artistic movement was born.

Leader of the Surrealist school, André Breton

October 1966

Soft-drink cans with ring-pulls are introduced to the UK for Prize Soft Drinks made by Stotherts Ltd.

6th Amidst growing concerns of drug abuse the US declares LSD illegal.

Grateful Dead took part in LSD trials

18th French cosmetics expert Elizabeth Arden dies.

19th Paramount Pictures is bought out by Gulf and Western Industries. Charles Bludhorn becomes president.

Elizabeth Arden, founder of the eponymous cosmetic company

21st Aberfan Primary School is crushed under an avalanche of slag as a coal tip collapses. 116 children and 28 adults are buried alive. Disaster struck as debris from the Welsh colliery was being dumped on the black slag heap – the National Coal Board had allegedly already been warned that it placed the village in danger.

A desperate rescue attempt at Aberfan

22nd Double agent George Blake breaks free from Wormwood Scrubs. Spy Blake, jailed for 42 years for espionage, makes his dramatic jailbreak by climbing a home-made ladder to scale the outer wall. Police suspect Soviet help in his successful escape.

George Blake

November 1966

Gustav Mahler

Gustav Mahler's *Second Symphony*, the first recorded with Dolby sound, is released in the UK.

5th 'Good Vibrations' by the Beach Boys enters the UK charts.

9th **Florence suffers severe storms** and the flooding of the River Arno. Millions of pounds worth of art treasures, including books, sculptures, paintings and photographic negatives, are destroyed or badly damaged at the Uffizi Gallery and the National Library.

The Beach Boys, playing in the 1970s

18th Czechoslovakian director Jiri Menzels' debut *Closely Watched Trains* is released in Prague. The reviews are favourable.

 20th Runaway spy **George Blake** reappears in East Berlin one month after his escape from prison.

23rd An international chess match between US and Soviet chess computers takes place...the Soviets win 3-1.

George Balke in Berlin

26th An experimental power station commences generation in France using the tide as a source of energy.

Florence after the floods

December 1966

7th William Walton's *Capriccio Burlesco,* conducted by Andre Kostelantz, receives its world premiere in New York.

The ill-fated Greek ferry, *Iraklion*

8th The passenger ferry, *Iraklion*, sinks in stormy seas off the coast of Greece. 280 people die.

12th The Amoco company announces yet more finds of oil in the North Sea.

The North Sea drilling rig, *Mr Louie*

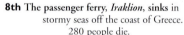

1966 sees the first episodes of *Star Trek,* a science-fiction television series set aboard the Starship Enterprise – a topical subject in the current Space Race culture.

15th **Walt Disney dies aged 65.** Creator of the cartoon character Mickey Mouse, Disney went on to produce *Snow White and the Seven Dwarfs*, *Pinnochio*, *Bambi* and *Fantasia*. He also brought his vision to theme parks, creating Disneyland and Disney World.

23rd **The last episode** of *Ready Steady Go*, the pop programme hosted by Cathy McGowan, is broadcast.

28th **Australia's tennis team** make it three Davis Cup wins in a row by defeating India.

31st **The Monkees'** 'I'm a Believer', written by Neil Diamond, reaches number 1 in the US.

1967

January 1967

1st **England's Sir Alf Ramsey and Bobby Moore** receive a knighthood and an OBE respectively.

4th **Donald Campbell dies** when an attempt on his own water-speed record goes horribly wrong. He was in *Bluebird*, on Coniston Water in the Lake District.

4th **Waif-like Twiggy**, who now earns 10 guineas an hour as a model, is tipped to oust Jean Shrimpton as Face of the Year.

Bobby Moore

The microwave oven is invented.

12th The UK's biggest new town, Milton Keynes, is to be created on 22,000 acres of Buckinghamshire countryside.

16th After 88 years of cracking adventure stories *The Boys' Own* comic folds as circulation falls.

22nd The Rolling Stones refuse to go on the traditional revolving stage at the end of their appearance on *Sunday Night at the London Palladium* TV show.

27th Three US astronauts are killed when their *Apollo* spacecraft catches fire on the launch pad.

The Rolling Stones

The Moog synthesizer is developed.

February 1967

12th **Two UK climbers** succeed in climbing the Matterhorn's north face in winter.

12th **Rolling Stone Keith Richard**'s house in West Wittering is raided by police looking for drugs.

Keith Richards charged

25th **The Beatles**' 'Penny Lane'/ 'Strawberry Fields Forever' enters the UK charts. It was recorded as part of the *Sgt Pepper* sessions at Abbey Road studios.

25th **The 'Boston Strangler'** Albert DeSalvo is seized by police 24 hours after escaping from a prison mental ward.

The Beatles pose for the press

March 1967

4th Queens Park Rangers are the first Third Division side to win the League Cup.

9th Stalin's daughter defects to the West.

Stalin's daughter, Svetlana Alliluyeva

19th After the **suspension** of London School of Economics undergraduate, David Adelstein, 1,000 students occupy the building. Adelstein had protested against the appointment of Walter Adams (the LSE's new director) due to Adams's connections with Rhodesia. After a 10-day sit-in the authorities reinstate Adelstein.

19th A 61,000-tonne oil tanker, the *Torrey Canyon*, runs aground near Lands End, in Cornwall. On 29 Match, the RAF drops bombs and napalm in an attempt to break up the oil slick.

The wrecked *Torrey Canyon*, still ablaze

April 1967

Barefooted British singer Sandie Shaw wins the Eurovision song contest with 'Puppet on a String'.

24th The Soviet cosmonaut Colonel Vladamir Komarov is the first human to die in space. The Soviets have denied previous claims of fatalities in their space programme. He died during the descent of *Soyuz 1* for, as yet, unknown reasons.

26th In London a **Picasso** fetches $532,000; a world-record price for a living artist.

Vladimir Komarov

May 1967

1st Elvis marries Priscilla Beaulieu. They were introduced when Elvis was in Germany with the US Army; Beaulieu was 14. After Elvis' discharge she moved to Memphis.

5th The first entirely UK satellite, *Ariel 3*, is successfully launched at Vandenburg Air Base, US.

13th The Bee Gees' 'New York Mining Disaster 1941' is their first UK single.

25th The Glasgow team Celtic is the first UK footballing side to win the European Champions' Cup. They defeat Inter Milan 2–1.

28th Lone yachtsman Francis Chichester lands in Plymouth, completing his round-the-world voyage. The trip took him 119 days.

June 1967

1st The Beatles release *Sergeant Pepper's Lonely Hearts Club Band.*

5th The start of the Six-Day War, between Israel and the Arab states: Israel launches surprise attacks by air and land.

7th The Queen meets the Duchess of Windsor in public for the first time since the Duke chose the Duchess instead of the throne 30 years ago.

10th The Six-Day War ends. Israel has taken ancient Jewish land from Egypt, Jordan and Syria. The cease-fire came about when both sides agreed to adhere to UN rules.

10th Spencer Tracy, US actor and star of *Guess Who's Coming to Dinner*, dies.

17th China explodes its first H-bomb.

19th The Jimi Hendrix Experience appear at the Monterey International Pop Festival. Already a success in the UK with single 'Hey Joe' and the album *Are You Experienced?*, it is the band's first successful appearance in the US, particularly their performance of 'Wild Thing'.

27th Barclays Bank introduces the UK's first 'Hole in the Wall' cash machine.

29th Rolling Stones Mick Jagger and Keith Richards are found guilty of drugs offences.

29th US actress Jayne Mansfield, star of *The Girl Can't Help It*, dies.

Jagger and Richards, guilty as charged

July 1967

The Hawker Harrier vertical take-off aircraft makes its first test flights.

1st BBC2 commences regular colour broadcasting...the service starts off with seven hours of Wimbledon!

3rd ITV launches *News at Ten*, a daily 30-minute news bulletin.

7th Nigeria launches an offensive attack on the military-run state of Biafra – it is two months since Biafra declared independence.

8th British actress Vivien Leigh, star of *Gone with the Wind* and *A Street Car Named Desire*, dies aged 53.

16th **London's Hyde Park** hosts a mass rally of at least 5,000 peaceful demonstrators calling for the government to change the law and make the drug cannabis legal.

17th **US saxophonist** John Coltrane dies aged 40.

23rd **British cyclist Tommy Simpson** dies at the age of 29 during the Tour de France.

27th **The National Guard** is called in to end three days of race riots in Detroit. Tempers flared over constant police harassment of black residents.

Attempts to resuscitate
Tommy Simpson fail

1967 sees the introduction of direct-dialling phone calls: from New York to Paris and London.

August 1967

Joe Orton watches rehearsals of *Entertaining Mr Sloan*

9th British playwright Joe Orton is beaten to death by lover Kenneth Halliwell. Orton wrote several popular West End plays including *Entertaining Mr Sloan*, *Loot* and *What the Butler Saw*.

15th The Belgian Surrealist artist Rene Magritte dies at the age of 69.

21st British legal changes see the introduction of parole and a decision that juries no longer need to be unanimous – majority verdicts are to be allowed in criminal courts.

27th Brian Epstein, who discovered and managed the Beatles, is found dead in his London flat.

September 1967

4th 17 ex-pirate radio DJs, including Tony Blackburn and John Peel, join the BBC for the launch of the new station, Radio One. It is scheduled to start on 30 September.

10th Spanish claims of ownership are rejected as Gibraltar residents vote overwhelmingly to stay British.

DJ Tony Blackburn

20th The 58,000 tonne liner *Queen Elizabeth II* (*QE2*) is launched by the Queen at Clydebank.

October 1967

Inspection of Che Guevara's body

9th Revolutionary Che Guevara is shot dead in Bolivia. An Argentinian, Guevara joined Fidel Castro's revolutionary movement in Cuba and after holding several government posts under Castro, left in 1965 to carry on his guerrilla activities elsewhere in South America.

12th *The Naked Ape*, Desmond Morris's revealing study of humankind, is published in the UK.

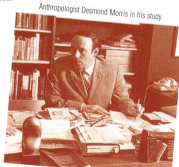

Anthropologist Desmond Morris in his study

13th Hong Kong is terrorised by over 100 Communist-planted bombs as the Cultural Revolution reaches the colony.

18th The Soviet craft, *Venera 4*, makes a soft landing on Venus. It is the first soft landing on any planet.

A computer-generated image of Venus' Maat Mons volcano

Cattle farmers panic as foot-and-mouth disease reaches epidemic proportions in Shropshire.

25th A bill **legalising abortion** in England is passed by the House of Commons despite vociferous protests.

The House of Commons

Flower Power hits the UK as the hippie culture gains momentum.

November 1967

A coronary bypass operation is devised by
Rene Iavaloro in Cleveland, US.

**Maxi coats protect mini
skirted girls** from the
autumn weather.

5th 90 are killed in a rail
crash at Hither Green, UK;
only 24 hours after 37
passengers died when a
plane crashed just outside
Heathrow.

8th The BBC
launches its first local
radio station – Radio
Leicester.

Police search the
wreckage of
Caravelle Jet

The first Laura Ashley shop opens in London.

Laura Ashley

9th Dutchman, Bernard Haitnink debuts as the principal conductor of the London Philharmonic Orchestra. Haitnink started out as a violinist before moving in to conducting. Previously he was principal conductor of Rotterdam's Concertgebouw Orchestra.

9th The rock and current-affairs magazine, *Rolling Stone*, is founded in San Francisco by journalist Jann S. Wenner.

19th The UK hits a 20-year financial low as financial speculation forces the devaluation of the pound.

23rd In London, Hubert Selby's novel *Last Exit From Brooklyn* is judged to be obscene.

DEVALUED—AND BA
RATE 8%
SUNDAY EXPRESS

IT'S DEVALUATIO
BY 14.3 PER CE
POUND IS
DEVALUED: IT'S
DOWN 14%
SUNDAY TELEGRAP

THE POUND DEVALUED BY
Spending Cuts:
Huge Loan:
Bank Rate 8 p.c
Sunday Mirror
DEVALUA

December 1967

Dustin Hoffman stars in *The Graduate*

Film premieres:
Barbarella (25th), *The Graduate* (21st) and *Guess Who's Coming To Dinner* (11th).

3rd The world's first heart transplant is performed by Dr Christiaan Barnard in South Africa.

9th Nicolae Ceausescu, 49, becomes Premier of Romania.

10th American soul singer Otis Redding dies in a car crash.

Nicolae Ceausescu, Romania's Communist leader

11th **After being held up** by inter-government squabbling, the supersonic airliner Concorde is finally unveiled in Toulouse. (The French call theirs 'Concorde' and the British, 'Concord'.) 16 airlines have ordered it.

14th **The Lawn Tennis Association** votes to end the discrimination between amateur and professional players.

17th **A massive search** for missing Australian Prime Minister, Harold Holt, draws a blank. He disappeared while swimming and is now feared drowned, or eaten by a shark.

25th Paul McCartney and Jane Asher announce their engagement. McCartney has been living with her family for almost two years.

1968

January 1968

The Beatles open their Apple boutique.

1st **The Irish-born writer Cecil Day-Lewis** succeeds John Masefield as Poet Laureate.

10th John **Gorton is sworn in** as Prime Minister of Australia after Harold Holt's assumed death.

Cecil Day-Lewis

Australia's new Prime Minister

1968 sees the launch of the world's first supertankers.

15th In the UK, a new divorce bill is published: the all-encompassing 'irretrievable breakdown of marriage' is now the only grounds needed for divorce.

15th Scotland suffers the tragic loss of 20 lives as hurricane winds batter the country.

16th Britons will have to pay charges for most medical prescriptions.

30th In Poland, students organise a demonstration to protest against censorship.

31st Trevor Nunn succeeds Peter Hall as the director of the Royal Shakespeare Company.

31st Vietcong launch Tet Offensive against major cities in South Vietnam and, for a while, hold the US embassy in Saigon.

Trevor Nunn with his wife, Janet Suzman

February 1968

The Royal Navy carries out its first test firing of the Polaris missile. The Polaris missile and its submarine carrier have been built under licence from US designs, but the nuclear warheads are of UK origin.

1st Priscilla Presley gives birth to Elvis's daughter, Lisa Marie.

Priscilla and Lisa Marie, in the 1970s

Decimal coins are introduced into the UK.

4th American beat-hero, Neal Cassady, aka Dean Moriarty in Jack Kerouac's *On The Road*, dies.

4th The first radio phone-in programme is launched in the UK.

17th John Lennon and George Harrison sign-in at the Maharishi Yogi's academy in the Himalayas.

17th In the UK, the Home Office steps up its fight against crime with the introduction of new legislation and the unveiling of an extensive advertising campaign, warning against the dangers of house burglary, featuring the slogan *Watch Out There's A Thief About*.

John Lennon with the Maharishi Yogi

March 1968

2nd The gigantic Galaxy transport aircraft is unveiled in the US. It is the world's biggest aircraft yet.

6th Three black Africans are hanged in Rhodesia (now Zimbabwe) despite all having received a reprieve from Queen Elizabeth II four days previously.

1968 sees the invention of the jacuzzi.

6th Singer Sandie Shaw marries fashion designer Jeff Banks at Greenwich registry office in London.

16th Senator Robert Kennedy (younger brother of JFK) announces that he will run for President of the US.

19th The West Indies lose to England by seven wickets in the fourth Test in the Port of Spain.

27th Yuri Gagarin, cosmonaut, hero of the Soviet Union and the first human to travel in Space, has been killed. Ironically he died whilst flying an ancient Mig 15 that crashed for unknown reasons. He will be buried in the Kremlin Wall.

31st US President Johnson agrees to restrict bombing of North Vietnam.

April 1968

4th A white assassin murders Martin Luther King.
Black civil-rights leader Dr King is shot dead in
Memphis where he planned to lead a march of striking
dustmen. In his last sermon he predicted his own death
asking supporters to remember him for giving 'his life
for love'.

Syd Barrett (front) with Pink Floyd

6th Syd
Barrett
officially
leaves Pink
Floyd.

7th Jim Clark is killed
in a crash during a
Formula 2 race at
Hockenheim,
Germany.

Martin Luther King
(centre) on the balcony
where he was shot

10th Stanley Kubrick's ground-breaking science-fiction film *2001: A Space Odyssey* is released in New York.

16th After months of wrangling the UK withdraws from the joint European Space Programme.

21st Tory shadow cabinet minister Enoch Powell forecasts 'river of blood' over immigration to the UK.

30th Frankie Lymon of the Teenagers, who sang on 'Why Do Fools Fall in Love' aged 14, dies of a heroin overdose.

Intel (Integrated Electronics) is founded.

May 1968

Bobby Charlton scores his 45th England goal to set a new record.

2nd French students occupy university buildings at Nanterre and Paris.

3rd The UK's first heart transplant is carried out at the National Heart Hospital in London. An 18-strong team led by Dr Donald Ross transplanted the heart into a 45-year-old male.

Dr Donald Ross (centre)

14th French students take over the Sorbonne university. They are opposed to their government's dealings with the US, in spite of the Vietnam War.

16th Part of Ronan Point, a 22-floor London tower block, crumbles to the ground. Three people die.

18th Richard Burton gives Elizabeth Taylor the world's most expensive diamond ring. It cost $305,000.

Demonstration in support of students, Paris

21st France grinds to a halt as workers go on strike in support of the students.

22nd The Church of Scotland agrees to ordain women as ministers.

22nd Manchester United beat Benfica 4–1 to win the European Cup at Wembley.

28th Alex Smith, the UK's first lung transplantee has died, just 12 days after undergoing the operation.

Mancunians welcome a victorious Manchester United

June 1968

Harrison Birtwhistle's opera *Punch & Judy* receives its British premiere at Aldeburgh's Jubilee Hall.

3rd US Pop artist and filmmaker **Andy Warhol** is shot and wounded by Valerie Solanis, a former actress in one of his films. Warhol undergoes five and a half hours of surgery after the shooting at his studio. Solanis surrendered to police hours later.

Andy Warhol in a New York nightclub

6th Senator **Robert Kennedy**, brother of the assassinated President John F. Kennedy, is shot dead in a Los Angeles hotel.

Robert Kennedy

112 nations take part in the Olympic Games, held in Mexico City.

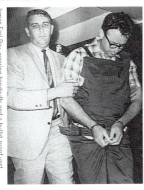

James Earl Ray wearing handcuffs and a bullet-proof vest

8th **Hunt for Martin Luther King**'s killer ends in London, with the arrest of James Earl Ray.

14th **UK motorways** receive their first automatic hazard signs on the M4.

24th **Birmingham-born British comedian Tony Hancock** commits suicide. Through radio series, like *Educating Archie* and *Hancock's Half Hour*, he developed his familiar character as a self-important, pugnacious misfit. The series moved to television but after ditching his co-writers, Hancock sunk into alcoholism.

Tony Hancock in happier times

July 1968

4th Greengrocer Alec Rose, aged 59, returns to Portsmouth to complete his 354-day round-the-world voyage.

6th Rod Laver and Billie Jean King become the first winners of the professional Wimbledon tournament.

Alex Rose after his 28,500 mile voyage

29th The Pope publishes his *Humanae Vitae* opposing any form of artificial birth control. Many Catholic leaders speak out against it.

31st The first episode of *Dad's Army*, a television comedy series about life in the Home Guard, is broadcast.

August 1968

1st Regular car and passenger hovercraft services commence across the Channel.

22nd Soviet troops invade Czechoslovakia to quash the reforming government of Dubcek and end the Prague Spring.

28th Warwickshire's all-rounder, black, South African-born cricketer, Basil D'Olivera, is excluded from the MCC's touring squad for South Africa, despite scoring 158 against Australia a week ago. In September he is chosen to replace Tom Cartwright – the MCC is banned from South Africa as a result.

September 1968

11th **The epidural anaesthetic** is introduced to relieve pain during childbirth.

27th **The decision by the Lord Chamberlain** to abolish stage censorship is followed by the opening of the American musical *Hair* at the Shaftesbury Theatre. The show which espouses free-love, drug-use and anti-Vietnam War sentiments features nude appearances by the cast.

28th **Mary Hopkin**'s 'Those Were The Days', produced by Paul McCartney, reaches number 1 in the UK.

Mary Hopkin, Eurovision Song Contest entrant

A photocall for the cast of *Hair*

October 1968

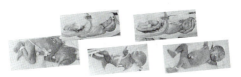

The surviving babies recovering in incubators

2nd The UK has its first set of sextuplets: born two months premature; five survive.

2nd With sales of over two million, the film soundtrack to *The Sound of Music* becomes the biggest-selling LP ever in the UK: one in four homes with a record player now own the record.

3rd Booker McConnell and the Publishers' Association announce an annual £5,000 literary prize for the best British novel – the Booker Prize.

6th British drivers Stewart, Hill and Surtees take the first three places in the US Grand Prix.

Julie Andrews in the *Sound of Music*

November 1968

President Nixon campaigns for the Presidency

6th Republican Richard Nixon wins the US Presidential election, eight years after losing to JFK.

18th Mervyn Peake, the British author whose works include the *Gormenghast* trilogy, dies aged 57.

21st US actress Jane Fonda, well known for her anti-Vietnam War protests, takes up the cause of the American Indians who have settled on Alcatraz Island.

28th Prolific children's author Enid Blyton dies. Her numerous works include the *Famous Five* and *Secret Seven* series and the *Noddy* stories.

Jane Fonda speaks on behalf of the American Indians

December 1968

5th The Rolling Stones release their new LP *Beggar's Banquet*. Custard pies are thrown at guests at the launch party.

Rolling Stones
Beggars Banquet

R.S.V.P

6th Out-spoken Tory MP Enoch Powell is 'gagged' by party bosses before making a speech on Rhodesia.

8th John and Cynthia Lennon divorce.

17th Mary Bell, aged 11, is sentenced to life in prison for the manslaughter of two small boys. The jury, guided by doctor's evidence that the killer suffered from a psychopathic illness, finds her guilty of manslaughter, rather than murder. Bell acted with a friend.

Mary Bell, convicted of killing two children

1969

January 1969

In the US, 20th Century Fox refuses to distribute Edoard Luntz's violently anti-establishment film *Le Grabuge*.

Newspaper magnate, Rupert Murdoch

1st A three-month struggle between Rupert Murdoch's News Ltd and Robert Maxwell's Pergamon Press ends with Murdoch taking over control of the *News Of The World*. The crucial factor in Murdoch's bid was gaining the support of the *News Of The World*'s majority shareholders, the Carr family.

3rd Civil-rights marchers end a 117-km (73-mile) trek from Belfast to Londonderry in violent clashes with the Ulster police.

Crowds scatter as police intervene in Ulster

15th Engine trouble holds up the *QE2* – it is still waiting for its first ocean voyage.

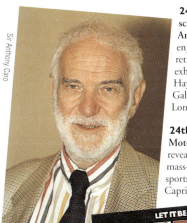

Sir Anthony Caro

24th British sculptor **Anthony Caro** enjoys a retrospective exhibition at the Hayward Gallery in London.

24th The Ford Motor Company reveals its new mass-market sportster – the Capri.

30th The Beatles play tracks from their forthcoming album *Let It Be* on the roof of the Apple building in Savile Row.

LET IT BE

February 1969

1st Fleetwood Mac hit number 1 with their new single 'Albatross'.

2nd British-born US horror-film star Boris Karloff, star of *Frankenstein*, dies.

3rd The Palestine Liberation Organisation has a new head, Yassir Arafat, to lead guerrilla attacks against Israel.

8th The Boeing 747 makes its maiden flight. This huge aeroplane has already been nicknamed the 'Jumbo Jet'.

British actor Boris Karloff

Children's television programme *Sesame Street* is seen for the first time.

11th In the wake of **Barbara Castle**'s proposed union legislation 'In Place of Strike', a strike, by the 1,600 female workers at Ford's Dagenham plant, proves successful – the women are awarded equal pay with their male colleagues.

Maurice Gibb and Lulu

13th Two **Cambridge scientists** succeed in fertilising a human egg in a test tube.

18th British Pop stars **Lulu**, who represents the UK in next month's Eurovision song contest, and Bee Gee Maurice Gibb wed.

Internet is established by the
US Defense Department.

March 1969

John Lennon and Yoko Ono begin their 'Love In'

Paul McCartney and John Lennon'wed: McCartney marries Linda Eastman (12th); Lennon marries Yoko Ono (20th).

2nd **Jim Morrison is charged** with six counts of lewd behaviour at a Doors concert in Miami.

5th **East End gangland bosses** Reggie and Ronnie Kray, both 35, get life sentences for murder.

11th **In the US, a cinema owner is imprisoned** and fined for showing *The Killing of Sister George*. The film, starring Beryl Reid and Susannah York as ill-fated lesbian lovers, had been proscribed due to its explicit sexual content.

28th Dwight D. Eisenhower dies.

April 1969

The impressive facade of London's Tate Gallery

7th In London, 25 **paintings**, including a Picasso worth around £300,000, are stolen from the home of the Tate Gallery trustee Sir Roland Penrose. A special detective force is formed to investigate the case.

9th British Concord takes off for its first flight.

18th Bernadette Devlin, aged 22, becomes Parliament's youngest MP. Her constituency is Mid-Ulster.

22nd Brother and sister duo, The Carpenters, sign to A&M Records.

23rd A Palestinian goes to the gas chamber for murdering Bobby Kennedy over his support for Israel.

May 1969

2nd Authorities are forced to shut down two New York universities after students riot on campus.

9th St Christopher is one of 31 saints being axed by the Vatican from the Roman Catholic calendar.

12th The UK voting age is lowered from 21 to 18.

16th The Soviet space probe *Venera 5* reaches Venus and sends back interesting data and photographs. The probe ceases transmitting just over a minute after entering the Venusian atmosphere. It is thought the probe was crushed by gravity.

22nd *Apollo 10* comes within 16 km (10 miles) of the Moon's surface before returning to Earth.

June 1969

20th High-grade oil is discovered in the North Sea. The feasibility of commercial exploitation remains to be assessed.

22nd US actress Judy Garland (Dorothy in *The Wizard of Oz*) dies in London. She was 47.

30th Biafrans face starvation as Nigeria blocks food aid. Red Cross relief flights are banned by the Nigerian government after claims that rebels in Biafra are using them to smuggle in weapons. Four million grow closer to death as the much-needed food and medical supplies stop.

Red Cross workers with aid for Nigeria

July 1969

2nd Rolling Stone Brian Jones drowns; the coroner decides he died of 'alcohol and drugs'. Days later the remaining band members play a free concert to 250,000 people in Hyde Park; Mick Jagger reads the poetry of Shelley in memory of Jones.

2nd In London, demolition workers find the paintings stolen from the home of Sir Roland Penrose in April 1969.

Brian Jones of the Rolling Stones

3rd The Byrds' single 'Mr Tambourine Man' enters the UK charts.

5th German architect Walter Gropius dies.

12th Tony Jacklin becomes the first Briton to win the British Open since Max Faulkner.

20th **Senator Edward Kennedy** faces questioning over the Chappaquidick Island drowning of his car passenger Mary Jo Kopechne.

21st **The USA crowns** a decade of the Space Race with a magnificent achievement. At 3:56 am BST, after leaving the *Apollo 11* Lunar Module, Neil Armstrong becomes the first human to set foot on the Moon. '...One small step for a man...One giant leap for mankind'.

30th **The High Court awards damages** of £33,600 to two boys left disabled by the drug Thalidomide. The drug was originally prescribed as a tranquilliser for pregnant women.

August 1969

The Newport Festival in the San Fernando Valley features The Jimi Hendrix Experience, Ike and Tina Turner and Joe Cocker.

Sharon Tate

9th Actress Sharon Tate, film director Roman Polanski's pregnant wife, is found butchered, along with six friends, in her Beverley Hills home.

15th British troops are deployed in Londonderry to protect Catholic areas from Protestant attack as sectarian fighting escalates. The Catholic area of Bogside is ringed with barbed wire. Troops patrol Belfast streets the following day.

17th German-born architect, Mies van der Rohe, dies.

Chaos in Londonderry

17th The last day of the Woodstock Music and Arts Fair at Bethel in New York. Torrential rain meant the site was declared an official disaster area, but with acts like Jimi Hendrix, The Who, Jefferson Airplane and Crosby, Stills, Nash and Young an estimated 450,000 people still attended.

30th Leeds FC's record of 34 undefeated matches ends with a 3–0 loss to Everton.

31st Bob Dylan and the Band headline the Isle of Wight Festival. Festival-goers pay £2 10s for the three-day concert.

31st Legendary heavyweight boxer Rocky Marciano dies, still undefeated, in a plane crash.

Bob Dylan's *Blonde on Blonde*

September 1969

Philips withdraw 'Je t'aime' by Jane Birkin and Serge Gainsbourg, after broadcasters ban it.

1st Rebel army officers under subaltern Gaddafi overthrow Libya's King Idris, 70, and proclaim Libya a republic. Crown Prince Hassan Rida publicly declares his support for the new regime.

Libya's Prime Minister Gaddafi

2nd Ho Chi Minh, President of North Vietnam, dies.

12th Air assault on North Vietnam by American B-52 bombers is ordered to continue by President Nixon.

21st The most prominent squat of the 1960s, at 166 Piccadilly, London, ends when police storm the building.

Napalm attack on Danang, Vietnam

October 1969

John Cleese and cast of Monty Python

The comedy show *Monty Python's Flying Circus* is first shown on the BBC.

16th **Leonard Chess**, founder of the Chess record label, dies of a heart attack aged 52.

21st **Jack Kerouac**, the American 'beat' author who wrote *On The Road*, dies. He was 57.

21st **Willy Brandt** is elected Social Democrat Chancellor of West Germany.

27th **A mass wildlife cull** takes place over 3,000 acres of Surrey, after two people are bitten by a rabid dog.

Willy Brandt, new West German Chancellor

November 1969

1st **Elvis** is at number **1** in the US with 'Suspicious Minds', his first chart topper in seven years.

11th **The UK and France** are to pay £3 million compensation for the environmental disaster caused by the stricken oil tanker *Torrey Canyon*.

13th **Ken Russell**'s film of D. H. Lawrence's *Women In Love* opens in London.

Women in Love, the film of the controversial book

1969 sees the founding of the Gay Rights movement in New York. It is triggered by riots after a police raid at a gay area.

14th *Apollo 12*, the second of the Moon-landing *Apollo*s is launched.

14th The first colour TV commercial is broadcast in the UK, by ITV.

19th A new force, called the Ulster Defence Regiment, is to be created in Northern Ireland under a bill backed by MPs.

25th John Lennon returns his MBE in protest against the UK's involvement in the conflicts in Biafra and Vietnam.

27th The Rolling Stones play Madison Square Garden.

The Rolling Stones relax in Hyde Park

December 1969

Film premieres: Fellini's *Satyricon* (1st), in Rome, and Gene Kelly's *Hello Dolly* (16th), in New York.

Members of the cast of *Hello Dolly*

10th Irish author and playwright Samuel Beckett wins the Nobel Prize for Literature. His plays include *Waiting For Godot*.

14th The Who perform their rock opera *Tommy* at the Coliseum Opera House in London.

19th Vasectomies can now be carried out under local anaesthetic for just £16.

23rd Flu rampages through the UK with a total of 294 lives lost in the last seven days.

24th Hippie 'Messiah' **Charles Manson** and three cult members are charged with the slaughter of American actress Sharon Tate and six others. Tate, the eight-months-pregnant wife of film director Roman Polanski, was found savagely murdered at her Beverley Hills home in August.

Harold Wilson

26th **Harold Wilson** is named 'Man of the Decade', with Enoch Powell as runner-up, in a BBC radio poll.

Charles Manson, as seen on a TV talk show

1969 Films:

Easy Rider
Midnight Cowboy

Index

COLLINS GEM
BABIES' names

COLLINS GEM
BEER

COLLINS GEM
BIRDS

COLLINS GEM
CALORIE
Counter

COLLINS GEM
FACT FILE

COLLINS GEM
FENG SHUI

COLLINS GEM
FLAGS

COLLINS GEM
Healthy
EATING

COLLINS GEM
QUOTATIONS

COLLINS GEM
SAS
Self-Defence

COLLINS GEM
SAS
Survival Guide

COLLINS GEM
SEASHORE

COLLINS GEM
TREES

COLLINS GEM
Understanding
DREAMS

COLLINS GEM
WILD
flowers

COLLINS GEM
WINE
Dictionary